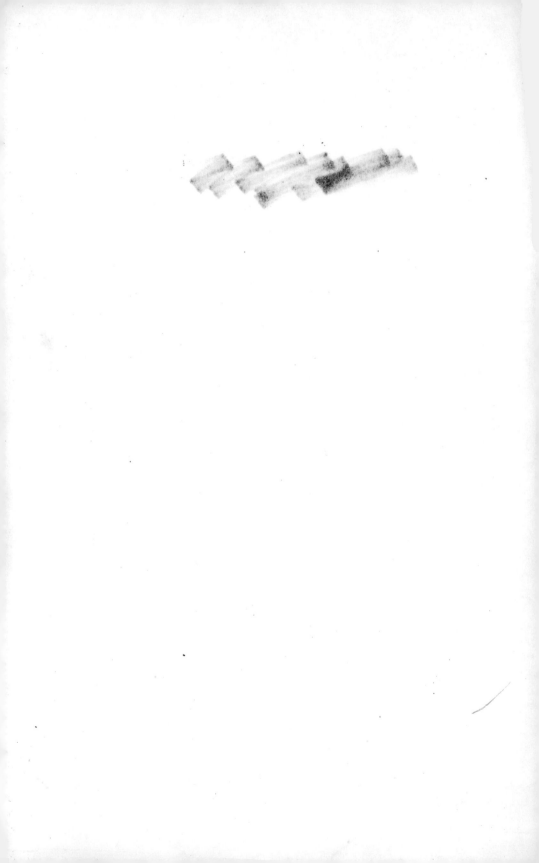

Record-Breaking Animals

The Hummingbird
World's Smallest Bird

Joy Paige

The Rosen Publishing Group's
PowerKids Press™
New York

Published in 2002 by The Rosen Publishing Group, Inc.
29 East 21st Street, New York, NY 10010

First Edition

Book Design: Michael DeLisio

Photo Credits: Cover © Mary Ann McDonald/Corbis; pp. 5, 12–13, 14–15, 17 © Joe McDonald/Corbis; pp. 7, 21 © George Lepp/Corbis; pp. 9, 11, 19 © Animals Animals

Paige, Joy.
The hummingbird : world's smallest bird / by Joy Paige.
    p. cm. – (Record breaking animals)
Includes bibliographical references (p.   ).
ISBN 0-8239-5960-0 (lib. bdg.)
1. Hummingbirds–Juvenile literature. [1. Hummingbirds.] I. Title.
QL696.A558 P34 2001

                                              2001000708

Manufactured in the United States of America

Contents

The Hummingbird

This is a hummingbird.
A hummingbird is a
very small bird.

5

Hummingbird Babies

Hummingbirds lay eggs in a nest. The eggs are very small.

A hummingbird baby
is tiny. This baby fits
on a coin.

9

Hummingbird Wings

Hummingbird wings go very fast. This helps them fly forward and backward.

11

Hummingbird wings make a humming sound. This hum gives the birds their name.

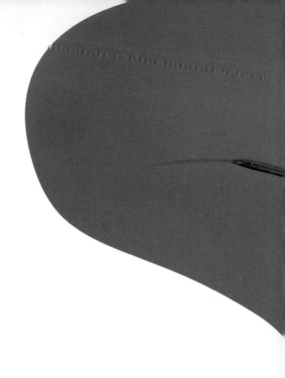

Hummingbirds can stay
in one place when they fly.
They can hover.

15

Hummingbird Food

Hummingbirds fly from flower to flower to get food. This food is called nectar.

17

Hummingbirds have long beaks. Hummingbirds use their beaks to drink nectar from flowers.

19

The hummingbird is smaller than most flowers. The hummingbird is the smallest bird in the world!

Glossary

backward (**bak**-wuhrd) opposite to the usual way

beaks (**beeks**) birds' bills

hover (**huhv**-uhr) to stay in one place in the air

nectar (**nehk**-tuhr) a sweet liquid found in many flowers

tiny (**ty**-nee) very small

Resources

Books

A Hummingbird's Life
by John Himmelman
Children's Press (2000)

Hummingbird
by Rebecca Stefoff
Marshall Cavendish, Inc. (1997)

Web Site
http://www.hummingbirds.net/

Index

Word Count: 113

Note to Librarians, Teachers, and Parents

If reading is a challenge, Reading Power is a solution! Reading Power is perfect for readers who want high-interest subject matter at an accessible reading level. These fact-filled, photo-illustrated books are designed for readers who want straightforward vocabulary, engaging topics, and a manageable reading experience. With clear picture/text correspondence, leveled Reading Power books put the reader in charge. Now readers have the power to get the information they want and the skills they need in a user-friendly format.